BUILT FROM CHAOS

Unlearning poison & reclaiming magic

By: ScIN

BUILT FROM CHAOS
UNLEARNING POISON & RECLAIMING MAGIC

First Edition:2026

Identifiers:
ISBN:[Paperback]979-8-951294-00-5
ISBN:[Hardcover]979-8-951294-01-2
ISBN:[E-Book]979-8-951294-02-9
Library of Congress Control Number: Pending
Cataloging-in-Publication Data available upon request.

Publication Details:
Published independently by ScIN

Art & Design:
Cover Art & Interior Illustrations: ScIN
Interior Layout: ScIN

For inquiries, community connections, or workshop requests:
ScIN.02@pm.me

First, I want to start off by saying thank you for taking the time to read "Built from Chaos." While this book is emotionally dense, it is with reason. As you go through each section, the mythological spine will come to life, helping you understand how they collide. If something hits too hard...take your time to breathe; jump back in when you feel comfortable to touch those topics inside of you.

In here, we will grind our teeth, happily cry from finally feeling seen; it will demand the truth, remind us of our personal magic, while seeing what it is like to live through personal/ancestral traumas.

"What I see, you see. What you see, I see.
We are one.
In this lifetime or the next,
We...Are...One."

There is a five-pillar architecture that will have a brief description to guide you on the movement behind each section.

Chaos. Zeus. Mortal. Yemaya. Lilith.

Chaos as the authority: before there was life, there was chaos.
Zeus as the ego: showing you who is in power. Mortal: the psychological feeling of being in the flesh.
Yemaya: gliding into the nurturing waters of the Orisha.
Lilith: choosing to no longer live in the shadows but to reclaim one's power.
You do not need to read BFC in order; you can choose what resonates with you.
Pick a page that calls to you on that day,
or read from the beginning to the end.

Trust yourself.

ScIN

Disclaimer:

BFC explores difficult and potentially triggering subjects.
- Physical violence
- Abuse
- Sexual assault
- Struggles with mental health
- Systemic injustice

These topics are part of a much larger discussion that is held in conjunction with survival, resilience, and healing in mind. While these poems are intended to help readers bear witness to these experiences, some readers may find them distressing.

****If you are currently experiencing trauma and mental health challenges, please consider reading with care.*
You have a right to step away, pause, and take a breath before returning.

Only return when you feel ready.

Need	Resources	Contact
Suicide/Crisis	*Suicide & Crisis Lifeline (US)*	*988*
Sexual Assault	*National Sexual Assault hotline*	*1-800-656-HOPE (4673)*
Domestic violence	*National Domestic Violence*	*1-800-799-7233*
Social justice/crisis interventions for BIPOC communities	*Call Blackline*	*1-800-604-5841/ callblackline.com*
Crisis hotlines (International) offer free emotional support anywhere/anytime.	*Find A Helpline (Inter national)*	*findahelpline.com*
Therapist for All	*Inclusive Therapy*	*inclusivetherapist.com*

We do not have to heal alone in the shadows...it is okay to seek help. Some pages may bring up complex emotions—processing with a friend or therapist can be a powerful step towards healing and understanding.

I hope these poems breathe magic back into you,
whatever stage you are in.

Table of contents

Chaos:

Destructive.

Exploitation.

Isolated.

Uninhabitable.

Stranger.

Unknown.

Gaslight.

Fertile Void.

The Great Unfolding.

Limbo

The dead is in here.

Do you feel that?

That dense, heavy air...
unmoved,
weighted,
almost too toxic to breathe.

It's lingering.
Un-passing.
Unaware
of what has just happened.

An energy
that once filled its body
is
no more.

It lingers.

Stagnant.
Heavy.

Dense to the weight of the room.

Smelling of baby powder
and decay.

The dead is in here.

The vessel

no longer inhabitable to the soul.

It finally malfunctioned
to the bones,
cold,
frozen in place.

But still,
the dead
is taking up
so much of this space.

What was once warmed with life

is
no more.

The soul
lost its area code.

Do you feel that?

It's so cold.

The Original Boogieman

Hello? Who's there?
No one.
Silence.

Hello? Who's there?
No one.
Silence.

Hello? Who's there?
I see you.
I am coming closer.

Shush...Shush...
Let me pet you here.

Shush...Shush...
It's okay.
I am allowed to do this.

Here's money.

See!
All better now.

Tell no one.
I'll be on my way.

" I was 7."

The Man

Would you like peace with that chaos, *Sir?*

Chaos was my friend and enemy

She was chaos.

And for a time, she was my friend
because I, too, took comfort in chaos
until it no longer suited me.

This version that values peace,
tenderness,
kindness,
sleep,
health,
honesty,
laughter, and joy
has overcome me.

I ignored it for so long
because chaos, at one point, was a part of me.
I wanted to see her through.
I wanted to help her,
but her chaos grew.

It was her choice.

A need to feel alive

in a soul that already danced with darkness.
A desperate soul
that struggled to survive in a dying vessel.

It was a choice.

A cry for help.

Chaos... she had no room for anyone else,
not even herself.

I needed to see myself
through the heavy doors of isolation to
find peace in me.

The chaos that vibrated high and heavy off of her
was no longer in me.

I was tired.

I was ready for peace
from what frayed my nerves.
Chaos can not be the only thing
that vibrates high
to destroy everything it sees.

A choice.
I had a choice to make.

I chose myself.
I had to choose the version of me
that I wanted to see come to life.

No longer will I choose
to be in the presence of a friend.

Chaos made that clear.

Ex Friend

How can we expect you to love us?

When you, friend,
hate yourself so deeply?
You lie and deceive your family and friends,
so things can work in your favor.

If they cannot do what you wish:
The venom secretes through your teeth.

Your children see all the bright lights with you.
But *what happens when they see the mask you have been wearing?*
The mask you carried to appear nice,
dominant,
powerful.
What happens when they see the person who would get love from the delusion and malnourished thoughts?
The delusion of what you should be
versus what you can be.

What happens then, friend?

What happens when they see the abuse you perpetrated
because of your own hurt
and inability to heal?

What then?

To deceive the world around you,

believe that your pain is the only true pain,
is the myth you have conformed to.

What happens when they see your greedy eyes,
craving attention from anyone who would give it?
The lies you tell yourself...
The hungry gaze of a man's attention to soothe yourself.

What happens when you realize it still leaves you thirsty for more?

The cup that is never full.
The cup that is always empty,
Expecting others to fill it with all of their energy.

Who do you love if you do not love yourself?

Who do you love if all you choose is hurt?

No Flow

Ease comes easily.
It is what the body knows.
It's the chosen flow.

Why do so many of us

choose to never let time go?

Ease is so diminished and dissolved—
we no longer live in flow.

That the chosen path ends up being
in

Chaos.

A rabid ego that lost all control.

Where has ease gone?
Why is ease removed to maintain this show?

who
or
what

is benefiting from this chaotic show?

Darkness

A corner.
A space.
So dark the eyes can't make it out.

It's the warm-iced thorned quilt
some choose to stay in
the *"woe is me"* feel.

The place that doesn't allow you
to believe in anything
other than your own pain.

It's weighted,
too heavy to lift off your body.

It keeps you tucked away at night...
a day...
a month...
a year.

"I am full."
"I'll wait."
"Leave me alone."

The
"Just one more time."

The

" I promise."
The

"I'm going to hurt someone because they did it to me."

kind of darkness.

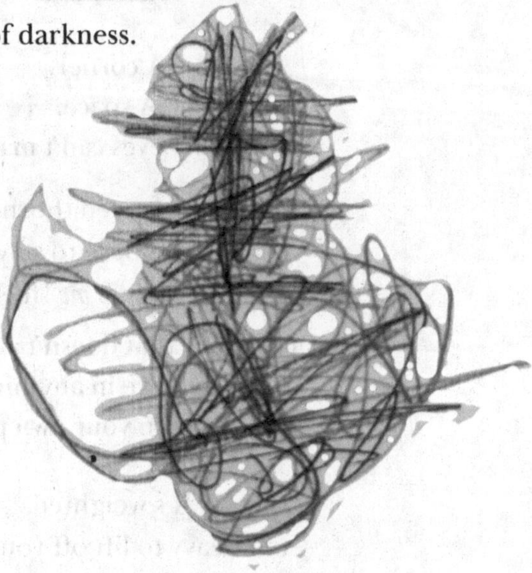

Privacy & privilege

After time was removed,
we ignored the signs and now,

It smells in here.

Like garbage left in the street on a hot summer day,
it's 99 degrees, and onions are slipping out
of this damp plastic bag
filled with old, raw meat.

Some walk by,
smelling of vetiver and sweat.

Ignoring the smell of privilege lingering in the air.

It smells in here.

The masking has a scent,
a scent

that no one is safe anymore.

P.25

In a home of shattered
spirits, molested cadavers,
dis-eased souls:

How do we fix this?

How do we unravel the cancer that has
woven itself
in and out
of the human experience
since before our time?

How do we collapse
the basic, unwavering mind
of an envy so deeply rooted
from the rich man's head
to the poor man's mind?

How do we do it?

World of Egos

For the life of me,
I cannot tell you where I am
or how I feel.

It's this torn
between two...
three...
four worlds of feel.

I am the observer
in a world of egos
and
egos have their own worlds.

I am torn with my world,
watching it go into effect,
watching it crumble
and become upset.

There's volcanic ash in the air
and turbulent waters.

But my world
is not theirs.

I am torn

between worlds,

and the fear of going crazy
is very real.

While I question mine
and my reality,
I also see theirs
in 3D.

Am I really the main character?

Are they the ***Dis-ease?***

The sickness of wanting
to be normal,
to be blind,
to act like they don't see?

Am I here
in this reality?

Or am I just a piece
of the puzzle
that was already at play?

I'm torn into pieces,
in different worlds,
where egos
are the main characters,
where freedom is make-believe,
and choice is not

what they see.

I am the pieces
scattered

into different worlds...
But:

What about me?

Suffer

The amount of suffering
we have seen is beyond anything
I ever thought to be real.
In the souls that pass us every day.

That befell us.
That hate us.
That love us.

That are free from anything to do with us.
I feel...
I feel your waking moments and losses.
These lives have seen too many dark days.

Scared I am for everyone,
in every world
and in every life we live.

To The Dancer Who Chose to Be Lazy

Who are you?

Do you know the wreckage
it took for you to be here?

Do you know the heartache,
the chaos,
every last shredded tear
it took for you to be here?

Who are you?

The question
that weighs your soul
against a feather.

The humanity of one
begs for another.

Who are you?

Drowning in your own beliefs

of what you think a society should look like,

without asking others

"What should our society look like?"

Who are you underneath
the cosmetically enhanced body?

The ill-informed mind?

Who are you trying to be

vs.

Who the fuck are you?

The person hiding
behind a phone screen,
smart enough to camouflage

into what "society" wants you to believe,

but dense enough
not to pick up a book
and read.

Too scared
to find the truth
beyond what you were taught.

It is the bomb
that will have all of us
on a bended knee.

WHO ARE YOU?

Not the fabricated version
of what you think we want to see.

WHO "THE FUCK " ARE YOU?

Because...

Because your words
will scar the bodies of your children,
wounds only your ancestors would know.

Because your ideology
will burn lifetimes of knowledge,
handed down from spiritual leaders before us...
just so you can blend in.

Who are you?

Because while you're screaming
at the top of your lungs
to be part of this...
this *"World,"*
You will never begin to understand
that you are not like them.

Your DNA is marked
by the people before you
who bled with fear in their eyes
from the ancestors of another.

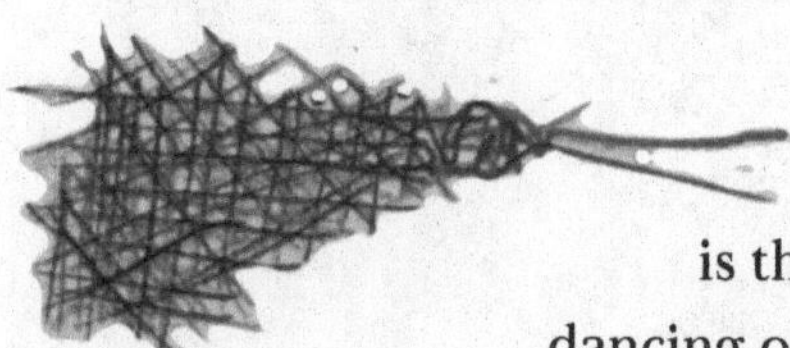

Your DNA
is the traces of slaves
dancing on each strand,
telling the buried stories
of rape
and
supposed freedom.

Your entire DNA
is the rage

of a million unhinged men

who took
from all of those
before your arrival.

So...
I ask again,
friend:

Who...
the fuck ...
are you?

Questioning the pity party

Did my troubled blanket of history
cause you to pity me?

Was it the worn-out holes and removal of my childhood
that gave you a sense of safety in your own world?

I was merely speaking of the existence of a past
that molded pieces of me.

That helped create the creature before you.

But I,
I never thought
that my truth would make you that uncomfortable
that your only resort was to pity me.

No acknowledgment of the truth.

Not seeing the complicated layers,
or
appreciating the person before you,
but to just leave room for pity.

Nothing else.

I just wanted to share that there are people

out there like me, too.

Taste of luxury

Maybe I wasn't supposed to be here.

Maybe...
I was just supposed to have
a *taste* of luxury.

Not to stay for dessert.

All of me does not feel at ease here.
Parts of me feel broken here.
Parts of me feel sleezy here.
Maybe the taste was the lesson and decision all in one.

Maybe I am just not supposed to be here.

Zeus:

Egocentric.

Negligence.

Dominator.

Counterfeit God.

Wrathful.

Power.

Patriarchal.

Self-serving Storm.

Narcissus Of The Heavens.

Zeus

Make them all blind,
and
then see how they really view you.

The false gods on the fake throne

We live on a floating rock.

You
and *you*
and *you*
want us to work,
but we live on a floating rock.

Surrounded by other rocks floating,
some glowing,
meteor showers,
some filled with thunderstorms,
clouds of gas and doom,
waters that are not blue,
massive black holes
that swallow every piece of light in their way.

And *you*
and *you*
and *you*
want us to work to stay?

You are killing life on this floating rock
for the fear of your gods and goddesses.

Your ego has gotten too big.
You're so infatuated
with the internalized, false world

you fabricated over time...
throughout time.

You cannot see,
we are living
on a massive, molded rock
with a core ready to explode.

Ocean waters have swallowed some of us whole.
Storms lose control.
Volcanoes are ready to erupt.

But your ego,
your ***EGO***,
is the one in control.

We are on this beautiful, massive rock
with lush green mounds
and waters filled with blue-green seas,

winds that carry the essence of our ancestors.
Stars seen from afar.
Flaming blue lights
before exploding into supernovae.

Lights glowing
to show the extraordinary night sky.

Worlds upon worlds.
Voids upon voids.

Layers upon layers.

Life upon life.

And somehow,
some way,
you think we should slave away

for your comfort.

The false gods living on the fake throne.

Glass-like pieces

There are pieces of me shattered on the floor
and you walk around as if it morphed to be your
throne.
As I crumble and fall to plea with the soul that is not home,
you look and stare at me as if
I were the one who imposed on you.

The audacity of this mortal to plead for honesty.
To plead for the recognition of humility.
The audacity for her to think us equal.
She should just be doing for me.

Grappling with the fact that I am in enemy territory.
That ***"I"*** was not equal.

I was but a toy for this person
who lost their soul a long time ago.
That I was but a piece to their play.
The storybook of their own victimhood.
My soul was a speck you wanted to crumble.

"How dare she walk around all bright? "
"How dare she be herself in the dark,
when I cannot even find my light."

As I crumble,
as I scatter my shattered glass like shards on the
floor, begging to be respected
and
seen as human.

Your dead stare

muted,

glazed-over eyes,
ignore my existence.
So, you can sit on the throne

of broken pieces of me.

Chokehold

I froze
for the mere understanding
that my life,
my life was not my own.

In that moment,
an entity can wrap its wickedness around you
and squeeze the life out of you.

In that moment,
my soul
was not home.

She floated out above me
to watch her vessel below her.

For the blip of a moment
to be squeezed by an entity
with no soul.
It was all dark ego.

Pressed against the warm body
that now ran cold.

Soul watched and registered again:

How can life lose control?

How the wrong energy
can wipe a piece of magic off this earth.

"I'll eventually return," soul said.

For now,
I have to preserve my magic
take this as a lesson.

For

never the *fuck* again.

Sister

I am mad at you.

I am mad at the fact that you can turn away
when it suits you.
That you think saving yourself is your privilege,
and doing anything more than watching
is too much.
That turning your back is the best solution.
That buying Starbucks
and prancing about your business
is productive to you.

I AM MAD AT YOU.

While people are being killed,
while children are being blown to bits and pieces,
while the system is crumbling before our eyes,
while day in and day out
people of color still have to fight for their lives.

I... AM... MAD... AT YOU.

My white sister.
The one who has helped me grow in many ways
but has beyond disappointed me today.

I am mad at you.

Your privilege of not knowing

what it is to be hunted,
killed,
and murdered.

Your privilege to have the balls to say,
"That is horrible."
Blank-eyed,
with a phone in one hand
and money in the other.

I AM MAD AT YOU.

For never knowing the struggle.
For not actually seeing what is right in front of you,
because the system still works for you.

I AM MAD AT YOU.

Because while I am screaming,
talking about my pain,

you return to act like none of it matters.
While genocides unfold before our eyes,
your response is,

"Let's go out."

I... AM... MAD... AT YOU.

White sister of mine,
because you have thrived...
lived off the culture
of Black, Brown, and Indigenous kinds.

Your favorite food.
Your favorite guy.
Your favorite style and updo.
That one Dominican guy.
That Puerto Rican one.
That Black guy
who showed you a world upon worlds
and now...

Now you're quick to turn your eyes.

I AM MAD AT YOU.

Because while I am struggling
to love the human race,
I am realizing we are,
and have always been,
in two different classes.

Your whiteness will always be your card up.
Your ability to blend into "society,"
masked into this dystopian universe.
Your ability to be blind on purpose
and still have...
support.

I am mad at you.

Friend of mine,
because the length between us
has just gotten that much further,
that much deeper.

We are worlds apart,
but on one world.
Dimensions a part
and still on one
plane.

Two rocks
floating in the solar system,
right by each other,
never able to touch.

I CAN NO LONGER CONFORM and BEND TO YOUR SOCIETY.

I can no longer act in my percentage of whiteness
to make you comfortable.
I can no longer unsee
what has been seen.

I am not a half,
but a whole.
I am whole woman.
Whole earthling.
Lover of night and light.
I am optimistic.
Joyous.

WHOLE.

Whole person.
Whole Rican,
in my African, Indigenous, and white side.
Whole earth

and one blood.
Whole in wanting to fight
for pure-blooded Indigenous kinds,
because they too deserve to live,
and not be taken down like mine.

Whole in believing in
humankind,
in liberating all of our minds
from the shackles of time.

I AM MAD AT YOU.

Friend of mine.
I want to take you to see
what a beautiful world can be
in this time.

But I fear

I am going to have to leave you behind.

Faded Ego

This friendship was only when it served you.
The long messages of wanting to hang
but never providing the space to do so.
Never having time.

Your time was the bottom of the barrel pickings.

Only when it best suited you.

Your existence only mattered when it was
a warm blanket to help soothe their ego.

You were always too busy.
At the same time,
you only had time to
hear your pain and stories.

The narratives you told yourself.
Only your pain was what fed the universe.
Booked and busy, no one else matters.

Deeply diving into social media
because that was what truly mattered to you.

Telling the world your every move
because the universe only fed on you.

The faded away friend.

I am a master of change

I am a master of change.
From the color of my skin,
to the hair that cascades around me.

I am the mood ring to my feelings,
my spiritual
and physical energy.

I am the master of many,
some, and none.

My ancestors blessed me with the
skin of a chameleon.
The shades of many.
The shades of all of them.
I am them,
the pieces,

The many kinds are all in the body of one.

My moods are the vibrant shades of hair,
blended into my personality.

While I am still me,
I am still all of them.
All are unique pieces of them.

I am the master of change.

While I still have not figured out all of me yet,

They know me.

All of me.

The new evolved version.

I am the master of change.

Chess piece

Do you see me?

I am seething.
Foaming.
Foaming at the mouth.

Raging.
Raging.
Raging underneath this tough skin of mine.
Because of you.
You are choosing to ignore me.
Ignore my pain.

My existence to you
is a third-class citizen.

I am just enough to work with,
but not enough to be viewed as
human.
I am just enough to work for you,
but not enough to have feelings.

I am
I am

A goddess in all of her might,
vibrant,
effortlessly beautiful,
calm and collected.

But with you,
I feel degraded,
abused.

The out-of-pocket comments
and
sideways glances.

I am nothing more than a toy
For your make-believe world.

To you,
To you,
I am just a disposable chess piece.
Not a king,
Nor a queen,
But ***a pawn.***

A pawn in your game.
A sleight of hand,
and I am gone.

Because to you...
To you
and all of your men:
I am not worthy enough to grace this
land because I have chips that have
peeled away the paint layers of my skin.

To you
my soul counts for none.

Do you see me?

My anger was inflamed by your words of belittlement.
Touched with a dash of shame.

I know what I am.
I know I am a goddess,
loving
kind.
I am worthy of so much more
than your ill-intended vibes.

But somehow,
you are the queen of this
imaginary game.

The one protected by all the king's men.

The one enchanted by the weight
of their wallets.

Do you see me?

Writing,
listing all of the broken pieces of society,
classless class level.

Frustrated.
Infuriated with a system
put in place to separate.

Separate all women.

I am too tired to fight

but too awake to act like I don't care
about the rage that fills
my heart of hearts.

The realization that the feelings
I was told to numb away
for my own good
a*re very real.*

They are here, taking up space
in my chest and head.

I feel shattered with regret for a life I never knew.

In pain.
Flawed.

Bruised with the regrets of my past lives rage.

What did I do to deserve this?
What did we do in our past lives
that made us this way?

Less of a human.

Not a queen,
nor a king,
but the mule of your abuse.

A stool for your dirty shoes,

while I wipe away years of my life,
working for the vain.

Idea of beauty

It's beautiful in here,
but it's not mine.
While I bask in the idea of getting used to this world,
I know "*This*" is not mine,
but it is very real.

That "*This*" can be taken away at any moment.
That any moment,
can be the moment
someone chooses they would rather see you suffer,
than face their own egos.

"*This*" moment can be taken away
just because
and that will have to suffice as
your truth.

To the distant relative

The "good" one.
The one depicted as in "Angels" the sky.
The all-mighty, powerful ones.
The wealthy ones.
The all-knowing, superior-race ones:

What have you done?

You have undone
what mitochondrial eve has done.

You have unwoven our DNA into separate
domains of
classless spaces.

The birth of one meant nothing to
you.
So, with the snap of a finger
you had it undone.

One life is worth less than another.

Unraveled
spun into intricate webs of hate,
envy, and dishonor.

None of us are "the chosen ones."

What have you done?

How have you validated this amount of
pain and suffering
to be the sum of your wealth.

How have you displaced your humanity for insanity?

A space with the essence of rape, robbery, and immortality.
Emptying souls for the gain of greed.
Never understanding that all life meant something.

What have you done?

Sincerely,
Blood of your blood.
Another distant relative.

Mortal:

Children Of Clay and Stardust.

Lacunal.

Vulnerable.

Resilient.

Legacy Of Flesh.

Unregistered Presence.

Ethereal.

Cognitive Dissonance.

Fragile.

Ice

Prickled skin.
Flesh gone tough.

Tight.

Frozen in place.
Piece by piece.
Space by space.

Stuck.

Unmoving.
Frozen.

I can't breathe.

Help me.

I cannot move.

Head?
Head isn't frozen.
Head, can you move?

Eyes can move.
But can she help me?

No.

Head does not have arms.

Head is useless.

Head is watching.

Head is registering everything.
The vessel is frozen in place.

Soul–
Are you there?

Can you see me now?

Soul

As I watch her frozen in
place, I see, feel
nothing but disgrace.

Violated for her.

Watching as she becomes a shell.

An empty shell
for a minute... or two.
That's all it took.

Watching.
Watching.
Watching...
taking notes.

I had to leave.

Must be safe.

Inside her was not safe.
It cannot be safe
If someone forces her energy to be
removed.
For now,
I watch.

I watch.

I watch until it is safe.

And then...

Maybe I will return.

Humanity

There are pieces of you missing.

Can you hear us?

Invisible

Can you see me?
I'm right here.

Can you hear me?
I'm right here.

Do I look familiar to you?
I'm right here.

Do you love me?
I'm right here.

Can you help me?
I'm right here.

Can you teach me?
I'm right here.

Please don't leave me.
I'm right here.

Please don't kick me out.
I'm right here.

Do you love me?
I'm right here.

Where am I?
I'm right here.

Kick. Kick. Kick. BOOM!

Why did she scream at me?
I don't know.

Was it my fault?
I don't know.

Do I look like him?
I don't know.

Why do I feel this way?
I don't know.

Kick
Kick
Boiling frustration.
Kick
Kick

I don't know why I feel this way.

Kick
Kick
Am I to blame?
Kick
Kick

Can you hear me?

Kick
Kick

I wish this were over.

Boom.

Make Believe

Gazing into the sunlit blanket masking the floor,
I ask:

What is life?

Untangling this make-believe world
with fake money used to keep humans in line.
I ask again...

What is life?

How complex it is to be a human being.
To do wrong,
to do right,
to do everything in between
and still question ourselves with:

"*What is right?*"

The further we go,
the more we think,
we understand the main question...

"*What is life?*"

As we chase the fake money,
the ideas planted in our heads to marry and carry,
still, we ask:

"What is life?"

As we watch our loved ones pass on,
and millions disintegrate beneath your bombs...
Still, I ask:

"What is life?"

We dig deeper into spirituality,
into faith,
into belief
to justify our ill doings to each other—
to disregard and disrespect one another.

Still, I ask:

"What is life?"

Do we continue to play the games
we've been conditioned to see?
Or
will we finally wake up
and ask the right question:

"What is life?"

In a room filled with people

I am screaming at the top of my lungs,
and no one hears me.

Nothing hears me.

Not a peep,
or a scratch of my skin
gets noticed.

Nothing.

Not a motherfucking bleep.

I am scared.
I am screaming.
Scratching.

So hard to breathe.

I am wheezing at the top of my...
my
lungs.

Trying to be heard,
but there isn't a bleep;
nothing comes out of me.
Because no one sees me,

No one hears me.

I am the being in the middle of this room,
voided out into the abyss of numbers
and considered inequivalent
to this room filled with people.

I am human.

Death

Unless you've been there,
unless you have experienced
it, seen it,
touched it,
tasted it,
felt it,
you would not know

or

understand the feelings that come after it.

The rude awakening that happens to your brain of...

That's it.
Never again.
I won't see them ever again.

It's these moments
where everything stops.
Things that meant so
much now mean so little,
or

nothing at all.

The world moves in slow motion.

Everything,
everyone
turns into a blur of light and dust.

You're alone in a pit of darkness,

watching the world move,
but no one knows
that the soul you were once tethered to
was ripped away,
severed to the very last tip.

Just
like
that.

Done.

Gone forever.

It's a nasty stench
that sticks to your skin like glue,
pungent and overbearing.

The stench of death.

Experiencing it.
Tasting it.
The awakening
of what once was
to what no longer is.

The jolt of electricity

bolting through your nervous system
into a reality that not many will
understand:

Death.

It shapes you.
It molds you.
It transforms a piece of you
either for the better
or the worse pieces of you.

But death...

Death

is the awakening
of the souls around you.

The Great Divide

Is walking into a store and not being treated the same.
Not having parents to claim.
The financial balance is not the same.
The tarnished account because of your last name.

The great divide is no meals in school.
Your parents are the ones to blame.
The...
"W*hy is your hair like that, when we should look the same?*"

The *"Where are you from?"* and *"Oh"* response.

The *"You're ghetto"* because your voice matches your frame.
The *"I'm watching you"* from afar to feel ashamed for existing.

Is the watching us die slowly from the poisons
dancing in our food,
while you brag about the $500 meal you experienced.
Watching me walk in with a medical boot and denying me access to a chair.

Is seeing my eyes puffed from distress
for you to ignore
because your problems conquer all.
Is thinking I don't deserve a seat at the table
because I don't meet your size requirements.

The understanding that you will not
take accountability for your actions
because it is everyone else's.

The divide is that you're too egocentric,
too self-absorbed to realize
that there is more than just you.

The divide is the brain filled with the black masses
of selfish entitlement and privileged behavior.

The divide is you.

Mirror

Here you are.

Damaged.

Destroyed.

Destined for failure because of who raised you.
Because of what you are.
Because of where you are.

The percentage that has not a chance of success.
No one believes in you.
No one believes you.

Here you are.

How are you okay?
What is wrong with you?

How are you OKAY?

In a Box

Am I to live in a pocket of niches
when I am layered with years, months, days, minutes, seconds
of *Life?*

The narrative you were told

My depth of perception is what they
avoid. So, avoiding me removes
the mirror in its place.

The mirror that forces them to look elsewhere,
to look inside.

My depth makes them
uncomfortable,
unknowing
Demi-gods to their make-believe worlds.

A Stranger on the train

I'm uncomfortable.

Because...
Because I feel the deep stare of your eyes
the empty blink,
with one agenda in mind.

The wanting,
yearning for a drink.
The empty sip
leading to your next high.

I'm uncomfortable.

Because the system put in place to tell you sweet lies,
lied about the help you were denied.

The deep, dark slope of nothingness
took over your mind,
washed away your dreams.

A hit here,
a hit there,
just to escape.

All of this.
This life.

That sweet,
otherworldly bliss,
that magical realm

where you swore you felt something before.
A drowning sensation of:

"I need more."
and
" I can't do this anymore!"

too...

"Where am I?"

"I'm uncomfortable."

Because we are standing on this packed train,
watching you dive into your next hit of empty lies.

Because...

Because this world is too much for your soul.

Your vessel
dimmed with nothingness,
a blink away from emptiness.

We continue to act
like you don't exist.

"Who robbed you, friend?"

***Who stole your innocence, will
to live in this world?***

Who took the many dimensions
you could have lived in,
with just a glimpse of help,
of healing?

I'm uncomfortable.

Because while we watch,
this too-packed train moves forward,
as you lay stretched across the chair,
lost in another world,
abandoned in this one.

I'm uncomfortable.

Because the soul in me
wants to reach out to yours,
pull it back into that vessel
that has suffered too much torture.

To wake it up,
to whisper:

"There is more."

I'm uncomfortable.

Because the line between you and me
is ever so thin.

Because the system that broke you
is slowly closing in on me, too.

And I...
I just don't know what to do anymore.

The light that once flourished in your eyes,
is dimming out in mine.

Not so long ago, I was
high on life,

now I am scared
for mine.

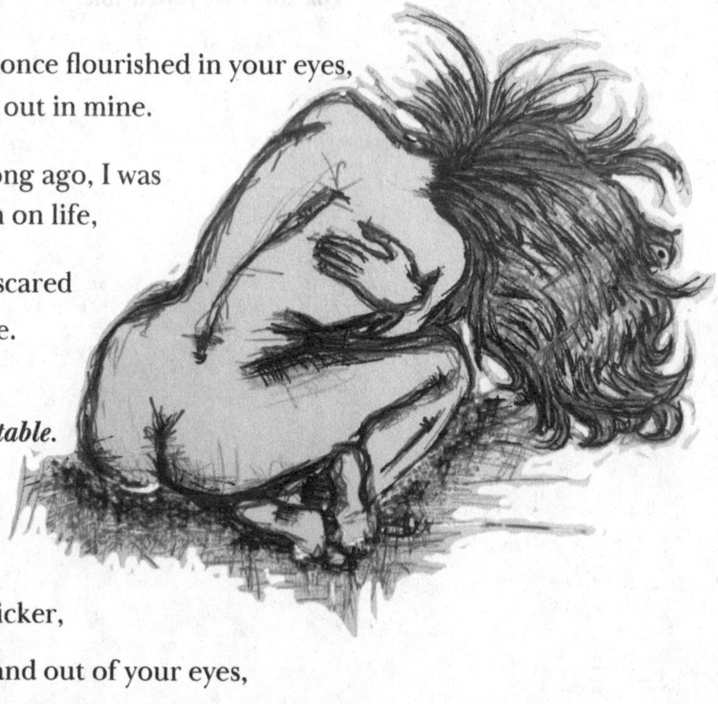

I'm uncomfortable.

Because I

can still see a flicker,

blinking in and out of your eyes,

but no one knows the quietness
that ties you to here.

That ties us here.

I'm uncomfortable.

Because the lies we were told

left a mark so deep,
none of us can see
what is the truth

and
what is a lie.
I'm sorry we failed you.

Text message

I hate this!

This...
This pounding in my chest
for not answering.

Not giving them what they think is right.
This guilt is overflowing in me.

A flood of anxiety filled my head
for not giving them what they want.
It stretches into my neck,
feeding the guilt of not being perfect.

Giving them the answer to their problems,
realizing mine was voided out
because I should not have any problems.

Gotta be professional
Gotta be kind
Gotta be wise
Gotta be honest
Gotta be patient
Gotta be what they want you to be.

For the fear of not being seen.
For the fear of not being worth it in a world
of haves and have-nots.

I hate this!

I hate this fucking anxiety!

Family or foe

When you were born into this world...
A world you did not request to be in,
are you automatically guaranteed loyalty
to the blood that is bonded to yours?

Are you to give
consistency,
loyalty,
reciprocity,
to the people unknown?
Only known through blood
or
Is it earned?

Earned in an equal manner.
The equal balance of love.

The choice between
I want to be here

Verses

I am here without a choice
but demanded to be.

Society tells us we have to be here,

Even if it involves the death of our souls.

Are we family or foe?

Eyesight

I do not want to be perfect.

I need my scars.
My big feet.
My evil left hand.

The scars that changed the pattern of my skin
to feed a memory of a moment I once was in.

If I get rid of it?

To the world, I would be the perfect nobody.
The person I don't want to be.

I understand the wounds
that built the person in front of you.
The person who experienced life
and
collected memorabilia along the way.

I know I survived,
I have a story to tell about a real person.
The seen-but-not-heard story.

I am perfect
With my new patterns.

My beauty is wounds and worlds deep.
My beauty is love addicted and love-sick.
My beauty is the imperfect scars all over me.

The reminders of the depth of a being
is not just seen but heard and felt.

Yemaya:

Guardian.

Saltwater Heart.

Ancestral.

Medicinal.

Restore.

Correct.

Sovereignty.

Matriarchal.

Fluid Resistance.

Tides Of Change.

Guardian of mine

Do you see me?

Do you see me untangling
the lines of our lineage?

Do you see me
maneuvering in my peace,
giving us space to breathe?

Ancestor of mine:

***Do you see the salutation of healing
and the fight to be seen?***

The drop of blood
that spreads thinner and thinner to
each of our members
and still,
you rise and fill me up
like the phoenix you are.

DO YOU SEE ME?

That deep yearning for love,
peace and freedom
still lives in you and transfers into me.

That power,
that energy
transmuted into something bigger,
something greater.

While I unravel
all that I am in this lifetime,
there are still memories
of belonging to the sea,
of traveling far and near,
of being blessed
by the air we used to breathe.

There are memories
of repression,
empty spaces,
massive voids
within me.

I have been here before.

Ancestor of mine:
I see why they fear us.

Because we hold the answers
they do not believe.
We hold the keys
to connect to this land.
We hold the magic
of being.

We are pure magic

in all forms,
and no matter how much
they try to wipe us away...
we are still here,
fighting to be seen.

Ancestor of mine:

Do you hear that?

That is freedom.

Bring us home.
You and me.

Ancestor of mine:

I hope I am making you proud,
because every last drop of me
is focused
on being free.

Blinded

May we lift the blinds that blind us.

May we take away the shadows that keep us in the dark.

May we shower in the sunlight with skin glowing
from her light.
May our thirst be filled
with ocean waters, salted and clean.

Show up

Take up space.
Take up all the space
to make them uncomfortable.

Show up as you are.
Live as you imagined your life to be.

Breathe in the air proudly.
Take up all the fucking space.
Because this is it,
one life,
this lifetime.

It should not be lived with the rules of society
on how you should look.

Your looks do not determine the soul
that fought tooth and nail to be here.

Your beauty is the light sparked inside of you.

Do not let them snuff it out.
Take up space.
Take up all the space.

Do not dim the light inside of you.

On Stage

In a sea of black,

this one just took a line,
this one has a gack,
and this one...
this one just got some smack.

In a sea of black:
I and I.
I and I.
I and I.

I and I am too nervous to understand,
but too wide-awake to erase
what I see in this sea of black
that is currently haunting me.

I am sweating,
mouth watering,
dry,
shaking in disbelief
that this sea of black is staring back at me.

Waiting.

Waiting for me to give them
the antidote to their pain in that
moment.
The quick fix.
The quick ease.
To heal every little reflective eye
in this sea of black.

I and I.
I and I.
I and I.

I am too scared to voice all of me,
because the imperfectly perfect sea
is judging me.

Either swaying to the beat of my drum,
or taking me apart at the seams before
I even hum a beat.

In this sea of black,
I am looking for my sisters,
my brothers,
my family,
my community to stand with me.

In this sea of black,
I am looking for hope, for joy,
for power in *you*
that turns into *us,*
and then we.

In this sea of black,
in *my* sea of black,
will you allow me to speak my piece?

The truth behind my beautiful black eyes
that have seen many seas.

Will we support each other,
watch our tides collide
into the most effortless, massive ocean waves
that create worlds of water for many seas?

In *my* sea of black,
are you now willing to hear me?

Give me a chance to show you
what unity could be.

Speaking to the robbers of ancestral lands

They speak in poetry of tongues
in ways you could not even begin to comprehend,
because you have chosen to deny
the existence of these men.

You have chosen to dismiss them
from their mounds and riches of
land.
To lie, to deceive these men.

They speak the language of lands before your time.
The poetic rhythm of life.
They speak the language of souls
that you will never begin to understand
because the absence of yours
drifted off a long time ago.

Their tongue is the rhythm of life on Earth,
in unison with the universe.
The effortless knowing of whose land it is
without a fight,
but a simple knowing.

Egoless and knowing.

Not just a piece

We are the sweet Indian.
We are the beautiful enslaved African.
We are the genocidal conquistador.

We are the dis-ease
that eradicated a piece of us,
for all of us to live.

We are the product of genocide.
We are just people trying to survive.

We are not a piece of those souls,
but a whole-
a whole lineage of eradicated souls.

Millions of black and brown souls.
Millions of stories untold.

A whole storyline,
washed and wiped away
because it did not,
it could not suit the narratives
of those who still live 'til this day.

We are the extension
that must keep learning,
over and over again,
because they are still
trying to take everything away.

We are too complex to understand.
So, they silence us instead.

But we are still the voices of the people;

echoing through the seas,
whispering through the trees before us.

The silent winds
brush against our warm skin,
consoling the many pieces of us.

All of us.

We are not a piece
but
a whole.

The mixed lineage
crafted not to survive.
The place they still hold in line.
The place that was never freed.

The piece.
The piece of our ancestors
that still lives in us,
but it is only amusement for
eyes to see.

A land robbed of its souls and gold,
used to nurture the dead
of those before us.

A piece of life
that hangs in a museum.

A piece...
A piece of...
A piece of all of us.

The stories untold because
they threaten their
underdeveloped emotional control.

It threatens them
that our wealth is in blood
has evolved into something more.

That our ancestors
still hold control through us.

That our "impure" blood
is the story of what theirs unfolded.

We threaten the diluted reality
of peace in their bloodline
because it is not the truth.

We are the stories
washed and wiped away
but
still told through our bones.

Through the sway of our hips.
The colors of our skin.
The curls that crown our faces,
to the privilege of
the ones that can blend in.

We are Taíno.
African.
Euro
not by choice
but by greed.

We
are many
complex
layers
of history
erased, robbed clean,
but never forgotten.

Guide

Mama
Mama
Can you hear me?

Can you hear me through the salty water
that flows from the open pockets in my eyes,
to my cheeks,
dribbling its way
down the corners of my mouth?

Mama
Mama

Mama, can you hear me?

Through the deep rumbling
rhythm of my heartbeat?
The thick blood pumping through
my straining vein?

Mama
Mama

Mama, can you hear me?

I am choking on my tears
with my heart racing a million miles a second,
through the pain I am feeling

And I
And I

And I cannot, for the life of me, feel all of this.

This numbing, throbbing ache in my brain.
Feeling confusion squeeze through my ears.

As I struggle to breathe.
I feel like I cannot breathe.

I can not
I will not.
I have not.
Remembered to breathe properly.
Too much.
Too much.
Pain.

Pain that brought me here.

Mama
Mama
I promise that I do not just call on you
when I am in pain.

I call on you to thank you, too.

I call on you for the love you give,
the love you gave me.

For the times you helped me to become
brave.

Mama
Mama
I know you hear me.

But for the life of me,
Why do I feel like I am going insane?

Mama?
Mama?

Okay...
I know...

Breathe, baby.
Breathe, baby.

You got this.
You will be okay.

You
Will
Be
Okay

Mama?

Thank you.

I love you.

Conditioning

I cannot believe
I believed that what was normal
was never safe.

A conditioning of the brain
slick and oil-like,
leaving remnants behind,
never fully cleansed.

What was cleansed?

Who was cleansed, growing up
in a home not of love,
but of a tainted, tortured one?

I believed that those beliefs
were normal.

That staying quiet
would grant me safe passage.

That allowing them to do what they
wanted with my body
was the way of life.

That adults were always right.

That the all-mighty,
powerful god,
with Zeus's might,
was untouchable.
All-knowing.
Law-abiding.
I believed that sticks, brooms,
and metal vases
being thrown at a child was
right and just.

That living in a nook in a corner
was right.

That whips to your left hand was right.
Because the devil did not,
could not
hold space here.

I believed that death
was the only plan.

That death,
and sadness,
and pain
were the only plans for humankind.

I can't believe

that I believed
light was just a bulb
attached to a wire
and not something within you
that can be snuffed out at night.

The conditioning was deep.

A deep conditioning.

One that was massaged into the brain
by the stylist,
making sure it was deeply saturated,
deeply hydrated–
with the wrong information.

I can't believe
what I thought was right.

But I found the right stylist
the one who learned my texture,

who helped me wash out the layers of grease.

Who taught me
the difference between what was given to me

and
What is truly mine.

The perfect amount of hydration.

The perfect amount of unlearning.
The perfect amount of ease and care.

To grow.
To unlearn what was slicked onto me.
To open my eyes
with the right amount of water.

To cleanse,
to clean up shop,
to be clear on the understanding
that beliefs can change, too.

That values can change.
That ideas can change.
That

their words are not law.

That adults are human, too.
That Zeus is the god in you.

So, pay attention
to the light they are aiming to snuff out.

That life always
has the opportunity to change.

To grow.
To do better.

To evolve.
To optimize.

That I...
I can evolve.

No matter what hand was given to me.

No matter what conditioning was implanted in me.

I can.
I will.

I will have a chance
to be part of something new.

I believe...
I am worthy

of starting anew.

Drowning

I am a grain of salt in warm waters.

A Drowning Legacy

I'm sitting in a hole buried beneath the
ocean,gasping for air.

Reaching up for coral,
any sign of life to nurture my lungs,
back to health.

I'm whispering words that are not complete,
because the ocean is grasping for air,
that once filled my lungs.

Astro projection or nightmare

I drowned in a nightmare.
Trapped as if it were real.

I drowned in the dark sea of emotions this morning,
thinking that this too had happened,
but it never happened.

Or

did it?

Was it another lifetime that

I was brought in to see how it played out?
Was my soul yanked out of her body
to view this shit?

It was too real.

What reality am I in?

Who am I?
Where am I?
How did I get here?

I am safe, I say to ***body.***
I am home, I say to ***body.***
I am in bed, ***body.***
I am in a space that is safe now, ***body.***
This is home for now, ***body.***

We are safe now, ***body***,

And that shit will never happen.

Because I still feel my heart racing,
chasing what was once real to me,
but it is not.

Or ***is it?***

It was but a dream that took too long,
and got carried away.

Drifted you into a plane of hurt,
tortured hearts,

decay.

The dream was too real for ***body***.

Body woke up anxious,
waiting for the shores to clear,
to fix the waves of emotions
that ***my body*** could not tell
what was real from what was fake.

Deeply fixated on the turbulent
energy of what may have been
another lifetime ago.

I am okay...

I say to ***body.***

We are safe, ***body.***

The opportunity to self-soothe,
to parental soothe,
has to be strong here.

Because
no one,

NO ONE

No one else can.
No one else will.
If I leave my life in the hands
of a stranger again,
my life will not,
nor ever be,
my own.

My life will be the dummy, the toy
for someone else's dreams.

The one no one sees.

The one faded into the backdrop of their play.
Lost in the dream of dreams
of what I could have been.

So I self-soothe.

Parental-soothe now.
Not out of fear,
but for knowing you are safe.

So, relax.
Meditate.
Do what you have to do
to get through today,

because it was just a dream.

Maybe not,

but it was just a dream.

I love you.

Today is going to be okay.

He cannot hurt you here.

For the Ancestors

When you were tied up
because of the ignorant blood of another:
What did freedom look like?

Was it the air whispering
through the beads of sweat on your skin?

Or

Was it the birds humming
to their own tunes?
Did the ground beneath you still feel alive?

Or

Was it dead energy
from the ones before you,
still struggling to survive?

What was freedom for you?

Was the only thing that ran freely?
The blood bleeding through the cuts that lay
all over you?

Or

The tears
that could no longer
hold space in your eyes?

D.

You are not a lake.

You are ocean waves
deep and chaotic
when you need to be.

Amazing and strong,
you steer ships
to the right seas.

You are more than just a piece
of this place.

You are a whole world
inside this ocean,
filled with wonderment,
vibrant colors,
and
different landscapes.
You are the driver
to your turbulent,
yet calming,
and beautiful seas.
You are not one,
but many.

You are oceans
deep in a man's body,
filled with beautiful dreams.

You are not a lake, friend.
You are the oceans
I dreamed about getting lostin.

The calm, soothing waters
that caress my skin,
and
the bed of water
I choose to drown in.

Freedom to live

Freedom is lying on your roof,
bathing in helios.
Listening to Gaia hum her tune onto your body.

Freedom is not a care in the world,
while not a soul watches you.
Letting the sun bless the melanin from your ancestors,
back onto your body.

Give me
that golden,
golden brown,
brown and beautiful glow.

Freedom is listening to the birds sing their song of life,
while the breeze takes hold of the air around you.

Freedom is feeling everything work together in unison,
flooding your senses with relief.
A sense of peace.

Freedom is the breeze carrying away
some of the curls that clung to your face
from the summer heat.

Freedom is not a care on this roof,
Just watching life move in all of its loudness and silence.

Freedom is the privilege of paying attention

and learning what ease can be.

My Grounding Stone

I have to touch him,
to feel alive,
to feel grounded.

To feel his warm body pressed up against the front of mine.
To feel his tiny back hairs nuzzle the front of my face.
Pressed up against his back in order to feel more
Grounded.

His warmth brings my soul back from the dreamworld.

The softness of his energy fills me
up and pours over all the pain
I felt through past lives lived.

His touch is that of an ethereal being
coming to give me grace and ease,
in the darkest weights of this world.

I have to touch him when I wake up,
because otherwise I would be stuck in the past worlds.
Worlds where no healing was in sight except the pain of
what never was.

He is my anchor in a living boat
while I linger in the dream world.

He is the warm fire of love

I am missing when I dance
in and out of the scenes of emotional horror.

He is more than what he is told to be

and

walks into this world with the armor of his own being
the strength of his intuition.

He is strength and magic.

He is the ease I never thought I would experience.

Lilith:

The First Rebel.

Powerful.

Androgynous.

Death.

Fertility.

Radical.

Untamed.

Equalist.

Matriarch Of Rebellion.

Advocate.

Unfolding Our Darkness.

Let there be light.

Let there be so much light
that they are blinded
by the actions of their ill doings.

Let there be so much light
that they are forced to see
what they have done in their dreams,
into the rest of their lifetimes.

Light...
the universal speed limit.

The speaker of truth
before you can even conjure up your
lie.

Touching each lifetime,
each corner of universal darkness.

Leaving traces of its remnants behind.

Let there be light.

For what comes to light is revealed,

and darkness can no longer overshadow
their ill behaviors or beliefs.

Let there be *soooo* much light that
they have no option
but to correct their ill doings
in this lifetime,
and the next.

May they know
what true loss and pain is.

Let there be light.

For this light is not your innocence,
but the universe
showing you
in all of your darkness.

It is the mirror
in front of you.

Reflecting to you...
your messy behaviors
and narcissistic truths.

It is the eye
to your storm.

The quiet, vibrant wake of nothingness
and everything
at once.

It is your truth.

Birth

My sin should not be because I exist.

Forgiven

If they clapped
while they bombed your homes,
Would you feed them?

If they bragged about taking
your innocence away,
Would you give them a fresh bed to sleep in?

If they trampled on your rights
and
left crumbs of your dignity,
Would you polish their shoes
to continue to walk on you?

If they starved your soul
made it their bitch,
Would you manifest nothing but joy for them?

Would you beg for forgiveness just for existing?

Would you mourn the puppet master,
While you lay on a bed of nails?

Would you forgive someone
with no remorse in their soul,
Just to have a false shadow of a day?

Would you believe in their god,

Even if it means erasing the one in you?

Projection

Talk to me.
Talk to me kindly.
Talk to me wisely.
But talk to me.
Do not project onto me
your pain and truth.

You manipulating
the situation to work in your favor
makes you...
Ugly.

The skin from your bones melts off
and I start to see you,
I see you,

All of you.

I see what you are doing,
and then
the question is lifted into the air for all to see,
Can I trust you?

Do not project your energy onto me.

You and I are not the same.
You are not me.
You have not experienced life in my skin.

To think I cannot see you,

Is the fool you are playing in your own world.

Your truth is for you to deal with.

Your pain is for you to heal.

Your projection of insecurities is not my own.
To think I cannot see the skin on your bones melt off,
leaving the raw flesh behind.
Please do not for one moment think I cannot see you.
Trust me,

I see you.

I miss her

I miss you.
The one who loved being held.

Who had sweet nothings whispered in her ear

and fell for it
every
single
time.

The solo champion.
Who loved being loved,
but couldn't find anyone
to love her the right way
or
at all.

Not enough to stay, that is.

I miss you
because you're open,
brave,
optimistic,
romantic heart
was eager to pull through for another day.

So, if it wasn't this one,
then maybe that one
would want to stay.

She waited tirelessly
under clear skies,

in her castle of dreams,
waiting for Mr. Right.

The knight who would sweep all her problems away.

The prince who would stay.
The king of kings,
worthy of this goddess.

Instead,
she was met with ***jokesters.***
After ***jokester.***
After ***jokester.***

Until ***the Fool*** card arrived
and came to destroy her day.

The Fool...
The Fool was me.
Us.
We.

Then came the Death card.

I miss her,
because without her,
I wouldn't be me.

This new phoenix
in a deck of shadows.
The ***surprise*** card.

The one where
I can be whoever I want to be.

I still crave
the part of me that died.

Because she was naïve.
Determined to feed herself romantic lies.

I miss being cherished.
Being honored.
Even if it was in the false arms
of *fake kings.*

Because now...
now I am so alone
in this cold, dark desert of dreams.
The deck is too clear
to see the next hand being dealt.

I miss the old memories of me.
Even if it was

just a dream.

I do not exist for your pleasure

I do not exist for your pleasure.

I exist to change this world,
to touch the lives that have not yet awakened,
to open the eyes that have not yet seen—
the ties that bind us.

I do not exist for your pleasure.

For I am pure magic in its rawest of forms.

My body bends and contours
to birth men like you.

My body changes to nurture life
in the most
simple and complex ways,
known only to women,
never accurately known to man.

I am not just here for your pleasure.

For I see far beyond
what your eyes will ever see.

My body bears souls.
My body nurtures them.

My body tells me all I need to see.

My gut is the tool
to see a thousand layers
without seeing at all.

I am pure magic
in its rawest of forms.

No matter how much

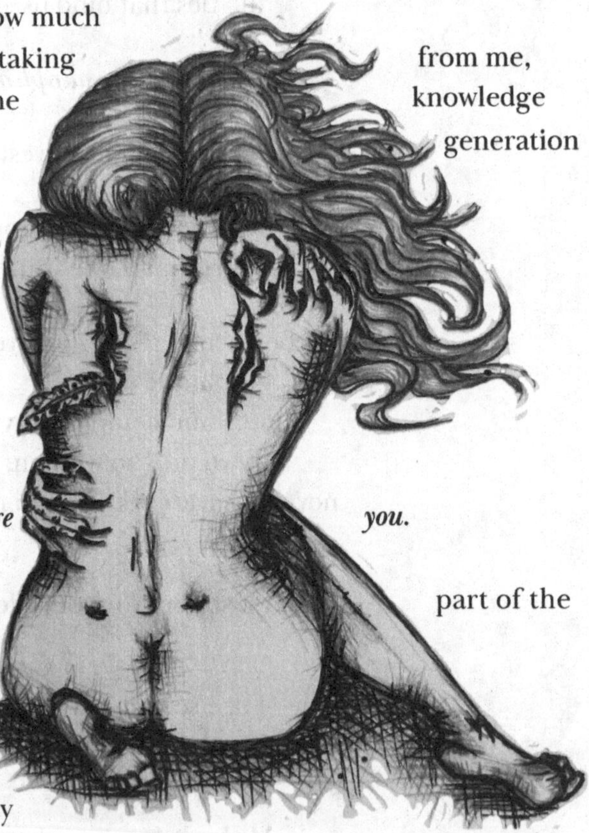

you think you are taking from me,
you are feeding me knowledge
for the next generation
to see,
to feel,
to understand
the blinded,
narcissistic entity
you have chosen to
be.

My magic should scare you.

My vessel is a part of the
piece,
but my soul...

My soul is the
pure, magical entity
that will learn, evolve, and master
what you could have never conquered.

Compassion.
Love.
Empathy.
Truth.
Joy.

Life.

My body.
Me.
Us.
We.

We are not here for your pleasure.

For we are pure magic in its rawest of forms.

And, you?

You will never conquer all of us.

The vessel is but a suit worn.

The soul is the energy unseen,
and only experienced by a few.

We *are pure magic in its rawest form.*

NO, I Mean all of Me

Here I am in the flesh.

The suit I wear represents the soul.
The complex layers that were conjured up
from my ancestors.

The illusion you built
isn't the multiple pieces of me.

The illusion is what you have chosen to see.

Do you hear me?
Do you hear my heart beating as yours does?
Do you hear my breath keeping me alive,
alive enough to start and finish the day?

Do you hear me sigh with relief when I am out of danger's way?

Do you see me?
Am I more than a skin tone or ethnicity?
Am I more than a voice?
Am I more than a pretty face?

No.

But do you see me?

All of me?

Belief

I do not consume the vision of
an all-mighty powerful one.

It is too much pressure for one being to carry.
To carry the weight of all others
and
not to live but die for others.

It is too much weight to bear.
The billions of souls who were given a shitty hand.

It is too much power to give.
To be able to bend so many in a box,
to conform
or
be penalized.

He did it right...
and she did not.
They did it
or
they did not.

The text complicated and mystified
to fit one type of man.

A book rewritten by man
over and over again,
but never the tongue of the beholder.

Traded in.
Changed to fit ordinary greedy men.
Behaviors of not "We" or "Us"
but just one.

One type of man.

My belief–
My belief does not hinder women.
My belief does not conform bodies to be toys.

My belief,
my soul's deep feeling is multiple verses
where each can stand in ancestral power.
Handed down,
diluted but alive and well, forever evolving.

My belief is in respecting each other's differences
and
giving power to our voices to sing in harmony.

Where choices are made through the vibration
through the energetic parasites living in our bodies.
Guiding you on what to do.

That we are created from stardust.

Where praying to the universe
is the universal practice.

The universe hears us echo through its dark space
and grants us safe passage,
after hearing the war cries of all of its children.

My belief is in the holy cosmos,
the great universe.

The pieces that are a part of us and never left.

The perfect storm to create us.
Made us.

The simple yet massive realization
that we are all one.
Riding this massive plane
and
trusting in the pain of our ancestors
to get us through most days.

My belief does not have to be set in stone
or
etched into the bones of our children.

My belief is mine
and
maybe yours.

Different gods for different purposes.
That can hold the weight of most tears
and reveal the ones that live in fear.

We are the universe within and out.
We are so much more than one man's
chaos.

I believe in us.

Your Heaven

If there is a heaven,
I do not want to go.

I do not want to stand in a place
next to someone who does not see me as an equal.
I do not want to live to build one man's kingdom
and die to build another dead man's throne.

To never live in peace,
but only to be accepted for the pieces of me
that are palatable.

If there is a heaven,
I will not pay for a plot of maybes
and make-believe prophet dreams.

Your heaven is not my heaven.

If there is a heaven,
I do not wish to stand next to the soulless.
To have fake niceties
filled with judgmental crumpets and tea.

People who would rather see children die,
than give them safety in a home.
They would rather see people starve than share bread.
They would rather put thorns on chairs instead of
planting trees to feed life.

I do not want to stand in your heaven.

Your heaven is a contract
signed with the devil
cosplaying as a power-loving being.

Your heaven tells me I am not equal.

Your heaven denies me wealth
based off of the mixture of my blood.

How am I to be loyal to anyone else but
myself?
To deny myself dignity because I do not fit
into the boxes of your heaven.

Your heaven tells me that my sin is wanting freedom.
To be treated equally is a sin of all sins.
Your heaven is
conditional,
non-loving,
unequal,

your heaven is rooted in
feeble man's dreams of Eden.

I do not want to be
a part of your heaven.

Asleep in my anger.

I woke up pissy.
Irregulated.
Dysregulated.
Discombobulated.
Dissociated from the world around me.
Mad at people acting like they cannot see,
will not see
the anger vibrating off of me.

I woke up resenting my peaceful nap,
my peaceful sleep, because the world is on fire
and I,
and I
feel like I cannot breathe.

I CANNOT BREATHE,
with the amount of anger vibrating off of me.

How?

How can we justify this much destruction?
Shrug our shoulders, say:

"Well, that is a part of history."

How can we mimic the same behavior as yesterday
as if a child isn't being raped,
beaten into sickness,
beaten into autoimmune dis-ease,

beaten into mental manipulation,
beaten until there is no more...
Us.

We
are
United,
interconnected
beings.

Energy,
living,
breathing
beings.

How can you deny what you've seen?

I woke up angry
because the dream was far beyond my reality.
It was far from the current version of me.
I woke up angry at me because
while I slept,
I felt the anger and venom
building up in me.

How can the colors of our skin make us less human?
Unworthy of living?
An abomination of human beings?
How can someone label you unworthy of life
because of what you believe?

How can someone see you and think:

"You're never going to be my friend."

Because I...
Because I...
Because I...

I AM the superior race, all-knowing,
and a part of ***GOD'S*** men.

How can you rape her lands?
her mounds of green and gold,
eruptions of oil and ash

then, say ***she is not worthy of breath?***

How can we sit in privilege?
and still feel helpless
when we are all supposed to be god's men.

I woke up angry!
That in a world with so many spiritual beings,
not one thinks we need to be down here to collect our energies,
to become one and light.
For all freedoms.
The high and mighty.
The chosen ones.
The spiritual bypassing.
The great,
large summoned gods and goddesses in us...
and still,
it's ***"peace... love... and light."***

Not helping the physical us.

The feeling...
The feeling of feeling free,
not just mentally,
but physically.

I woke up mad today.
And part of me blames me,
because I have been
dysregulated,
and a savage
for only realizing the little world around me.

I woke up today.
But now...

I wish I were still asleep.

Dream world

Sometimes they feel so real,
I can touch them.

I can feel the feeling as if
I lived them another lifetime ago.
I can feel the judgment of your eyes on my body,
as if I am waiting to be touched.

I can feel the manipulation rolling off of your eyes,
landing on your lower lids onto your lips.
To molest your mouth to the next hurtful
roll of your language.

I can feel the stares burning the tiny fibers of hair on my skin.

It is so real that when I wake up,
it's hard to tell where I am.

Am I in this reality or the next?

Is this life a dream, and when I sleep, is it reality?

When I close my eyes,
I feel the shame of having you back in my life.

To feel the anxiety of my strength
being ripped away from me in different realities.
Different scripts of different places,
but the same scenes
and same faces.

Were we lied to?

Are we walking in the dream world of our own
perception of what life could be like,
and the real world is when we close our eyes.

To pick the reality we next want to live into?
or
Are our minds that good at tricking us
into replaying the last lives we danced in—
with different :
"Lights. Camera. Action."

I can feel the distortion of the room when I wake up.
The softness of this dark room starts to feel more alive.
An eerie, dense, heavy energy lingers around my head and body.
As if I time-traveled and needed help adjusting to this room.

I left my body behind while I danced in different worlds.

As I sit here in this dark space,
with the softness of the air lingering around me,
things slowly start to become real.
The table in front of the bed comes into its shape.
The sun peeking through the shades.

Still,
I sit here in the dark,
wondering:
Did I come here willingly?

I question all the thoughts
of what true reality is,
and if we are all just time travelers in dreams,
conjuring up our next reality.

I question all of it,
as this space starts to settle in,
the pictures on the walls become more detailed
and the plush couch in the corner never looked so new to me.

My heart still feels the pounding
of the world I once was in.

My heart feels like it was played with
tossed heavily back into my chest cavity,
as if it were a baseball on a dusty field
being hit back into its rightful place.

As if a shooting star was ripped from the sky
and landed in my body,
still burning with the night.

I question,
What is this reality?
Am I really in one?
Or
Am I dancing in between worlds?

Can I ask you a question?

When did you decide that I was not good enough?
When did you decide that my curves were just for pleasure?

That my skin was meant to be mutilated by your touch,
that my hair was to be played with
by your jealous hands?

When did you decide that I was just for play,
and not to be seen or heard?

When did you decide that my magic
was to be manipulated into you,
energy taken for the beast within
so you can thrive and live off of my magic,
to live off of your sins?

When did you decide that I,
a creature of might, strength, beauty, and power

was
not

good enough?

Rude behavior

May I help you?

With that targeted gaze on the tip of your eyes,
touching the rim of your lashes

ready to come out of its sockets.

May I help you?

Yes,
You with the judgmental sway of your head
and the tight-lipped snare that's directed my way.

MAY I FUCKING HELP YOU?

Loose Blood

If we do not stand for the freedom of all,
we will never be free
from the whips and chains
that have already been in place.

Remove the blindfold that they placed.

Rinse your eyes with the blood of your ancestors;
see what they have seen.
Rise, blood of mine.

Rise.

There is no "just" you or I.
There is all of us.

We have endured the rape of our innocence,

our culture,
our homes,
our lands...

To be left with nothing?

Your outspoken word
will be perceived as rebellion and terrorism
for breaking the chains

that bind you.

So be it.

Be free, little bird.

Be free

In the way your ancestors
wanted to live.

Be free in the way Mother Earth has taken up space.

Be free like the wind caressing every tree branch,
every leaf,
every building
and
sea.

Be free like our ancestors used to be.

Before we were manipulated into thinking Mother
does not heal.

That what Mother has provided was
uncivilized, animalistic, and ill.

Be
free.

Your own personal hell

I cannot tell you how,
but there is a knowing
of *fear*,
of ***hate***,
of ***hurt***,

and an understanding of why you do not like me.

My loudness.
My hair.
The DNA I am wrapped in.

I hate that you do not see me.
I hate that you choose to ignore me.

The one who carries the same organ
on the outside of her body, like you do.

The human in me is not enough.

The one whose blood runs garnet
under her skin,
just like you
and
bleeds red.

I hurt for what a life could be.
What respect could look like.
What understanding could be.

But there is envy in you, friend
that runs deeply.
I am starting to think it is a mutation.

While you study and mutilate...
our bodies.
It's you seeking validation in us,
because your flaw is the hate you carry.

The envy that burdens you so much
that holds too much space in the place you call "home."

The chaotic one,
that you do not know how to tame.
The seat of your consciousness.

I hurt for the time we were free.
Truly free.
Free to be on the earth
floating in space in this universe.

Free to eat.
Free to live.
Free to breathe.
Free to just ...

Be.

I hurt for the understanding that
no matter how much I scream
and reiterate my rage,
you will not understand.

You will never understand the pain
our ancestors lived
and bled over into this generation.
The wound that was left open.

No TV show,
No movie,
No book,
No partner,
Can prepare you enough
for what was robbed from us.
The lineage you cannot see or find.

Just feel.

You feel that generational trauma
that lives in your bones.
It is your reality.
I hurt for the souls before me.

But most of all,
I hurt for you, friend.
I hurt for your ignorance.
I hurt for your mutation.
I hurt for the mere understanding that
you will never be free
from the demons that live in you,
that robbed you of your dreams.

I hurt because while I am learning to navigate this world
in all of its woes,

you will never learn what true freedom is.

Because the more you rob,
the more you kill,

the more you envy,
the more you try to destroy me,
us.

You
Will
Never
Ever

Be free.

Your own personal hell is you.

Before I was alive

Before I knew myself,
I knew to stay quiet in a room
full of strangers.

Because my energy was to be muted.

Before I knew myself,
I knew to chase paper
without knowing its origin
or
how it is used to keep us in chains.

Before I knew myself,
I knew the darkness of the ones who birthed me
by two colors

Black and blue.

Before I knew myself,
I knew through my DNA
I was considered non-human,
but a piece to lay with.

Before I knew myself,
I knew that those in position to tell us who we are
were never in position of knowing
who we are.

Before I knew myself,
I knew
the *fire*,
the *death*,
and *fury*
It took to get here.

The Corners

There is a silence when you understand your shadowy corners.

The corners are filled with hidden secrets
and pockets of joy.

The corners that were robbed from you,
in return given back empty spaces.
The corners that once glowed with pieces of magic
are now empty.

The pieces of you that were dimmed.

Muted to wash away all the color that attached itself to you.

The things that kept you alive.
A heavy quietness lives there now.
No longer what it used to be.

It is the evolution of you.
What you once were and what you now have become.

To rebuild.
It was something cleaned away and buffed
for new spaces to grow.

It does not mean you are dead.
It does not mean you have to let it consume you.
It just means you have more space to grow now.

Breaking the curse that you
"can't evolve past this."

Is breaking the generational curse.

Healing what once lived in the shadows
is learning to live
and live without them.
Learning to evolve past them.
To evolve even when your shadows are exposed.

Submit to a god

Am I to submit just for existing?

Deliver myself,
my body,
my soul,
my mind,
just because they do not value my bloodline.

A forced plague given to those before us,
should not be all I am worthy of in this lifetime.

It should not be my "***deliverance***" to struggle and die.

There is a blinding fury for the parents who birthed me,
because of the selfish need to keep up with a fake society.

To blend into the idea that we are all equal.
To not prepare your offspring for the world
that does not want them to breathe.

It is cruel behavior.

Am I to submit
because the truth in me
believes that love, peace, and unity can be real?
That the magic in us is real?
That the blood that runs through me,
does not define all of me?

That the soul in me
knows these wars
are suppression based on ill-founded beliefs?

On books that cannot possibly define all of us in this world.

The judgment
of "one
magical
being"
and all his
jealous men,
should not be my
death sentence from the
moment I am born into this life.

Am I to submit

All the pieces of me
in order to allow their dis-eased bloodline to win?

Sin of a Parent-Son of a B!t>h

Our parents gifted us dis-ease
with bodies not granted a chance to survive.

They became the abused to the sinner,
the sinner who chose to abuse.

Take away their right to ease.
Take away their right to sleep.
Take away their right to peace, because
the dis-ease in me has too big of an ego
to allow children just to be.

Give them pain, they said.
Give them no mercy, they said.
Give them lies.

For the lies will absolve them of their sins
when Sunday comes.

Our parents gifted us dis-ease for existing.
Now,
How do we heal the unhealthy?

How do we live a stress-free life when Chaos
was our stepping stone into this world?

May their sins end with us.

May dis-ease leave our tiny bodies.

So, we can have a chance at peace.

May we be granted a chance to win at life.
May we speak up for ourselves in the dark,
where fingers crawl.
Where dreams are stolen
and
silence is the poison of choice.

May we be granted the full opportunity to
heal from the sinner who lied their way into
the temple of our bodies.

Old Friend

I guess this is where our story ends.

The privilege of being the perfect shade,
In the eye of the destroyer,
created a space where nothing can live.

I have a question for you:
What if we were blind?

Would you be able to taste the difference in our blood?
Would my heart beating faster than yours be the giveaway?
Or
The touch of my hair?
What then?

What if we were all blind?

What then?

Acknowledgement

It's important to note that I am still learning as a poet/writer.
I lived a life, and pieces of me dance through each word that I share with you, but I would not have been able to do this without the people and experiences I have been given.

The people who have shone a light on my flaws—the people who tried to snuff the light out of my body.
The lessons I learned, good and bad ... thank you.
You showed me how powerful I really am.

I want to give the warmest and most fulfilling thank you to my partner Dmitry, for believing in me wholeheartedly even when I crumbled at the seams—giving me grace when no one else would and encouraging me to keep going. Your love has nurtured something deep in me that I did not know was missing.
I love you. I am forever grateful to have your light in my world.

Vanessa Dreme, you—are— a—goddess.
Thank you for keeping my voice consistent and showing me that my truth matters. I am grateful for your patience, kindness, and dedicated work.

Angela Ramil, I would not have been able to see this side without your help. You opened up a world in me I did not know was dying to live. I saw the pain and hurt through our sessions, but I also saw the beauty of what a world can be like if we decided to wake up. Beyond grateful for our time together. Thank you.

To whom this book calls—I see you and hear you. Thank you for seeing me, too. While our time is brief through these pages, I kept you in mind every single time I touched my keyboard to bring this book to life.

Some of us stay silent for the fear of the world's crushing hand,
and in return, our magic blossoms through
the darkness. Keep your feet grounded and head
on tight.
We have work to do.

This is just
the
beginning.

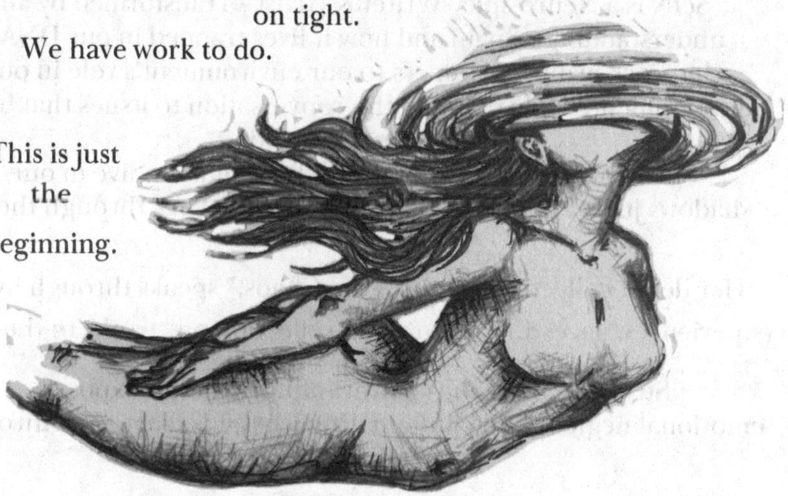

The Voice

ScIN is a Neuro-spicy Writer & Artist—Transformed by an understanding of pain and how it lives trapped in our DNA.
Her work brings awareness to our environment's role in our development, while opening the conversation to issues that have divided us for too long.
She believes beauty, along with freedom, can live in our shadows just as much as our light—once we work through them.

Her debut collection, "Built From Chaos," speaks through lived experiences, ancestral trauma, and reflection on "truths to the lies" we tell ourselves.
Stripping away the comfort of normalcy, it exposes emotional neglect while illuminating what it is like to live through systemic isolation.

"The mirror is left on the table. Will you use it or walk away?"

-ScIN

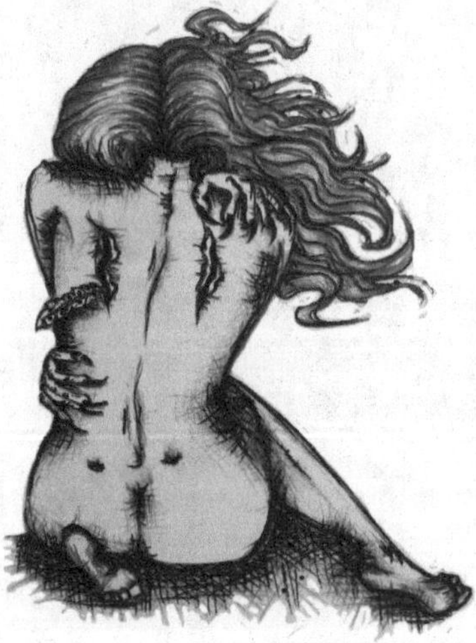

www.ingramcontent.com/pod-product-compliance
Lightning Source LLC
LaVergne TN
LVHW040519210926
848480LV00007BA/1518